GW01033383

The Tree

Sally Teggart

AuthorHouse™ UK Ltd.
500 Avebury Boulevard
Central Milton Keynes, MK9 2BE
www.authorhouse.co.uk
Phone: 08001974150

© 2010 Sally Teggart. All rights reserved.

No part of this book may be reproduced, stored in a retrieval system, or transmitted by any means without the written permission of the author.

First published by AuthorHouse 6/1/2010

ISBN: 978-1-4490-7679-5 (sc)

This book is printed on acid-free paper.

Once upon a time there was an estate set in the midst of the most beautiful gardens. The inhabitants of the great house were a Father and his Son. The house was impressive; it sat facing north with windows that offered a vista to every area of the grounds. At the back of the house was a sprawling conservatory, and to the left of that was the magnificent walled gardens and the nursery. To the right of this was situated a patio that was a riot of colour in spring and summer. The front garden was a north facing slope that lead up to a high plateau, and here the master of the house had planted heathers and dwarf conifers that nestled into the slope of the hill avoiding the especially cold winds that blew during the winter months. The rest of the garden was comprised of lush rolling lawns set with strategically placed flowerbeds that were home to a colourful variety of flowers that bloomed in their own season. Special little pathways beckoned the wanderer to various places of interest among the estate; one in particular led to a quiet gazebo where the setting of the sun could be viewed in all its splendour in the quiet and cool of a summer evening. Every kind of tree and flower flourished in the garden.

One day the young Master of the house was strolling in the garden. He looked around at all the trees, shrubs and flowers, the result of years of careful planning and back breaking work, a work of co-operation between the three of them: his Father, the gardener and himself. They were pleased with their work. Trees had been planted in some places to give shelter to plants that flourished beneath their shady boughs, and in other places they had been planted just for their beauty. Shrubs dotted the garden here and there to provide a focal point to a particular area, and of course there were flowers, lots of flowers, simply for the sublime enjoyment of their colour and heavenly scent. The three of them had lovingly tended the garden, seeing to the needs that each plant required for healthy growth.

That day the Master had decided to plant a tree at the top of the hill in the front garden. Down in the nursery the Master chose the young sapling he wanted. He picked a young plant that would eventually grow into a great tree. This tree promised an impressive parade of seasonal glories. In late spring, clusters of creamy blossoms would burst forth in glorious profusion against the fern like foliage. Then, as the season turned, the young green leaves of spring would mature into the rich dark green foliage of summer, with a slight gloss to their faces that would give them a lasting fresh look. Flamboyant bunches of small scarlet berries would then bridge the change over from summer to autumn, and the leaves would first turn yellow, then red, and finally a blaze of gold.

The little tree was delighted to be chosen by the Master; she had been waiting for some time to be planted out in the garden. She knew she belonged to him, and thus he could plant her wherever he willed, but she rather fancied a little flowerbed beside the conservatory where she could be near to her friends that still stood in their pots in the nursery. Also, at that side of the garden, she could enjoy the long hot summer days and have shelter from any inclement weather. But the Master planted her at the very top of the hill at the front of the house.

At first she quite liked it, although she missed her friends. The view was heady from there; she could see – well almost – the whole garden or at least what she thought was the whole garden. The Master and the gardener were very attentive to her that first spring they planted her out of her pot. The gardener watered and fed her, and the young Master would come and talk to her, encouraging her to grow. She heard them talking about her as they worked in the garden nearby, and the Father said that if she put her roots down deep she would be okay. At first it was strange not being in her pot and it took a bit of getting used to; she had to work really hard to put her roots down, but on the whole she enjoyed it. After all, this was to be her new home, she told herself, her place in life, so she settled down to the routine of life out in the Master's garden.

Then, one year at the end of summer, a terrible storm struck. The little tree was blown about so fiercely that some of her young twigs were broken off. She lost most of her leaves and felt even her roots moving; she felt certain she was going to die. When the storm was over, the little tree assessed the damage. Oh, she felt so bedraggled; she had so few leaves, so many broken and damaged bits. She looked around the garden, and from what she could see, she was convinced that she had fared worse than any other tree or plant in the garden.

"That must have been the worst storm in living memory!" she shouted to the nearest heather.

"Yes," he agreed, "a bad storm indeed; we're a bit exposed in this part of the garden, but I've known worse. When the north and east winds blow, things can get pretty scary here."

The little tree shuddered at the very thought of those cold winds.

She spent the remainder of that summer struggling to put her roots down deeper into the rich dark soil in preparation for the next storm, which according to the heather would surely come. She survived the long cold winter, dark as it had been, and once again, the promise of spring was hers. She was shocked and unsettled however, when the same thing happened to her in this delightful season as she had endured last summer: she had just started to grow when along came a storm that nearly blew her to pieces. She did the only thing she could do: she dug down deeper with her roots until the storm passed, and then she recovered as best she could until the next storm would come along, *which it certainly will do*, she thought bitterly, having now been taught the difficult lesson that storms were not a one-off occurrence.

One year there was a particularly nasty storm that seemed to spring up from nowhere. By this time the little tree had faced the fierce north winds and lived to tell the tale, but this storm was different; everything in the garden seemed to be affected, burned and scorched, blown level by the east wind. The little tree lost a lot of her new growth to that storm. While everything else in the garden recovered and grew and flourished, filling the estate grounds with their colour and perfume, bringing much pleasure to the occupants of the house, she spent the rest of that summer in a sorry-looking state. How the little tree longed to be in one of the flowerbeds beside the conservatory or even back in her pot in the nursery; anywhere would be better than this place.

"Why was I planted here?" she cried out to no one in particular. Surely the rest of the garden were talking about her, maybe even laughing at her; she looked so pathetic. She *knew* that she was meant to grow into a great tree, but every time a storm blew, she lost leaves and branches. She began to worry that maybe her growth had been stunted from enduring so much hardship. Although the gardener visited her after every mishap, she noticed that he did this with everything growing in the garden, making sure that all was well, but the young Master seemed not to pay any attention to her anymore. She worried that perhaps he was disappointed in her.

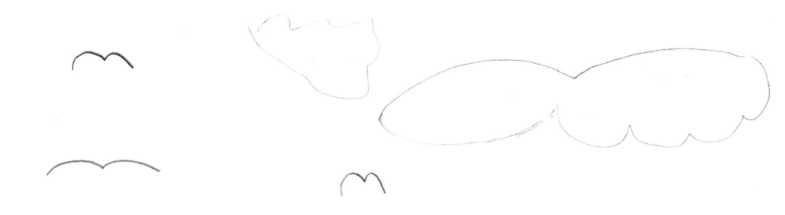
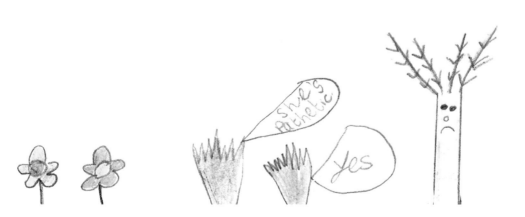

This was the pattern of the little tree's life for several years. She felt as though she lived in a perpetual state of setbacks and disappointments, but she never forgot the words of the Father that she had overheard in the garden when she had first been planted out: "If she puts her roots down deep, then she will be okay." And so this is what she did.

The little tree managed to keep the growth she had made as well as add to it, despite the storms that tried unsuccessfully to level her. Then, during her perpetual winter (the term she had given to the last few years of her life), and almost unnoticed by her, she had grown to maturity. Her roots anchored her deeply and securely in the same spot of ground where she had first been planted; her branches were strong and full of leaves, and the flowers she had produced that spring had filled the garden with fragrance. It was now nearly autumn, and her branches were filling with scarlet berries clustered together in neat ranks among the leaves.

Despite the strong sense of security she now had as a fully mature tree, she still pondered that unfathomable question: *Why, I wonder, did the Master plant me here in this particular spot?* She could see the Master walking in his garden enjoying his beautiful creation. He came up to her smiling as he always did. She decided she would ask him this question today.

"Why did you plant me here, Master? It has been such a struggle...."

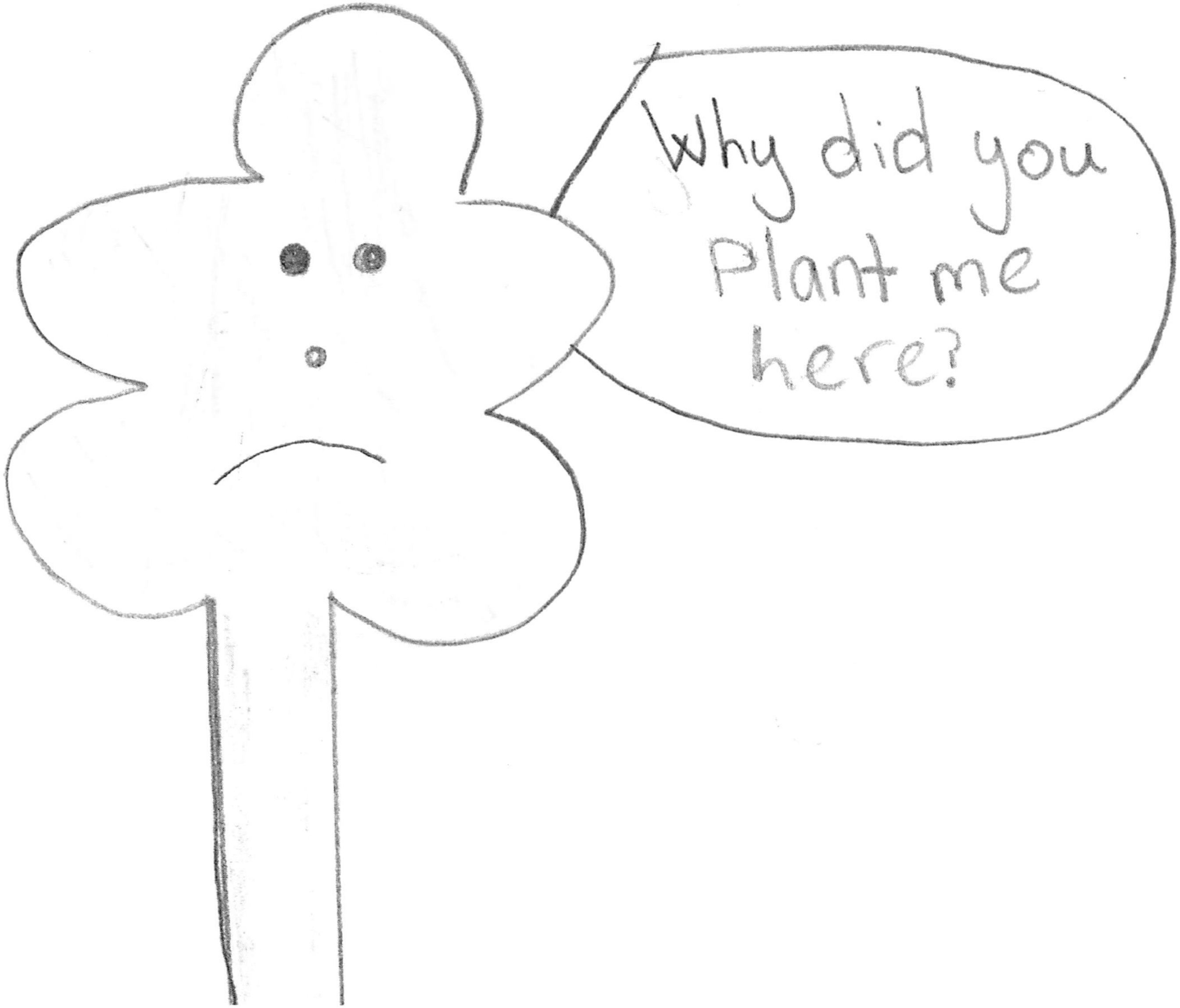
Why did you Plant me here?

He looked lovingly at her and replied, "We wanted a tree that we could look at from the front window of my Father's house, a tree that would have beautiful flowers, scarlet berries and leaves that turned crimson in the autumn. We needed a tree that would be hardy and could take the storms that blew, especially the winds from the north and the east.

So I chose you, because no other tree would have grown and blossomed in this part of the garden where I planted you."

The Master turned as he heard his Father and the gardener walking up the hill to join him by the tree. They all stood smiling at her, nodding in approval at her strength, her beauty and her growth.

"Ah," the Father said, "she has become a beautiful tree of righteousness, just as we knew she would."

You are the shoot I have planted

The work of my hands

For the display of my splendour

Isaiah 60-21b

About the Author

My name is Sarah but everyone calls me Sally and I live in Larne in Northern Ireland.

I am a mother to one daughter and granny to one granddaughter. A committed Christian

I am an accredited local preacher with the Methodist Church in Ireland.

I enjoy walking gardening reading and music. Now I haven't time for any of these as I have discovered writing. I love to travel especially the outward journey.